Passenger Network
Map included

Passenger Network
Map included

How to run a RAILWAY

This series, of general reading interest, also has an eye on careers. It explains how service industries, in contrast to manufacturing industries, are run. Each is concerned with an activity that touches the lives of most people, and which employs many thousands of workers. Here are explained the 'secrets' of success in one service; how the complex web of movement and activity reaches the public at many points. How does a letter get to Timbuktu? How does a plane land safely in a storm? How does a railway, with merely a three-minute train interval, avoid smash-ups? How does a ship find its way from Melbourne to New York or London? And what kind of shipping fleet do you want to run anyway?

Titles published and forthcoming:

How to run a POST OFFICE
How to run an AIRPORT
How to run a CHAIN STORE
How to run a BUS FLEET
How to run a RAILWAY
How to run a SHIPPING FLEET

All of these books are reliable and up to date, have been vetted by experts in their trades, are written in lively, narrative and participant fashion, and contain many pages of plates. Where necessary careers guides and glossaries have been added.

General Editor: Sally Brooks

For books about the manufacturing industries please see the IT'S MADE LIKE THIS BOOKS, published by John Baker.

How to run a
RAILWAY

F. George Kay

JOHN BAKER LONDON

Published in 1971 by
JOHN BAKER (PUBLISHERS) LTD
5 Royal Opera Arcade
Pall Mall, London SW1

ISBN 0 212 98405 5

Printed in Great Britain by
THE MILLBROOK PRESS LTD, SOUTHAMPTON

Contents

Acknowledgements

The author expresses his thanks for the help of the personnel of British Rail, who patiently described their duties, and to the officials of the Board in London and the Regions who supplied data and specific information on the past, present and future operation of the railways. Special acknowledgements are due to the Press Officers of the Board who read the script and made valued suggestions and amendments, and to the engineers of the Société Nationale des Chemins-de-Fer in France about the world speed record test runs.

Illustrations

The photographs are reproduced by courtesy of British Rail, London Midland Region; British Rail, Western Region; and the British Railways Board

CHAPTER 1

The track

That railways revolutionised the land transport of heavy materials was not solely due to the invention of the steam engine but to the much earlier adoption of a track on which a wheel could run smoothly. The unchallengeable advantages of the rail over an ordinary surface, no matter how carefully laid, are that it reduces friction between moving wheel and the stationary surface to a minimum, eradicates the obstacles of bumps, and, perhaps more important once mechanical power became available, it becomes an automatic steering device: the railed vehicle goes wherever the track leads it without guidance by the driver.

The invention of the rail is lost in the far past of human history. In a crude form it must have followed closely on the invention of the wheel: someone realised that flat stones placed beneath the two wheels of a wagon made movement easier. Certainly the Athenians knew about the benefit of grooved stones as early as 1500 BC when they laid a track of them in order to haul their boats across the 3½-mile-wide Isthmus of Corinth.

Probably tracks of this kind were in use whenever heavy materials had to be moved, as in the mines where stone for Egyptian pyramids, Roman temples, and early Christian churches, was quarried. Miners eased their formidable task by raising the track above the ground instead of laying it flat or cutting a groove into it. This raised track necessitated an edge, or flange, on the wheels to act as a guide. The carts of the Middle Ages copied the wheel span of Roman chariots used centuries before, and modern trains follow the same gauge, now standardised at 4 feet 8½ inches in most countries, except the Soviet Union, where the gauge is 5 feet.

The early rails for flanged wheels were made of wood, then of cast iron plates nailed over the wood to minimise wear, and eventually of cast iron. But this metal either broke or was worn away comparatively quickly and by the time mechanised trains were becoming heavy and moving quite quickly it was necessary to use the more expensive wrought iron, which was not so brittle as cast iron but still had a useful life of only a few months. The invention of processes to make steel cheaply solved the problem. Steel rails were in use by 1857.

Strong as steel is, it cannot sustain the stress and weight of a moving train without a special foundation. This has to spread the load, remain dry and compact whatever the weather, and provide a resilient, cushioning effect as the moving weight of the train wheels passes over it.

The bed on which the rail track (always called a road by railway-men) rests consists of three layers. The lowest, the formation, is the base on which the special bed is laid. It consists of levelled material obtained from the locality – sand, chalk, gravel, broken rock, and so on. It may be quite thin if the natural terrain is hard and stable, but can consist of immense quantities of transported material on boggy ground, for embankments, in areas of clay, and similar un-stable material.

Above the formation come two layers of ballast. The lower one consists of hardcore extending the whole width of the formation. It is composed of fairly large pieces of stone and rock, heavy enough to take the weight without moving, but full of crevices so that water quickly drains away. The upper layer of ballast directly supports the sleepers. It usually consists of rock chippings or slag, tightly packed so as to prevent the sleepers moving laterally, or 'creeping', which is movement longitudinally in the direction the train travels.

Sleepers used to be cut from high quality timber, impregnated with preservative to prevent rotting and destruction by insects. The heavy cost of regular renewal of millions of sleepers made from imported timber – there are normally more than 2,000 sleepers to the mile of rail – resulted in experiments with steel and concrete, and stressed concrete is now widely used.

Concrete sleepers are not much cheaper than timber ones, but of course they are much more durable. There is a still newer kind of track in which concrete paving is used, laid by machine in the same way as on airport runways and motorways. There are neither sleepers nor ballast, and the rails are fastened directly to the concrete slab.

A glance at railway lines in two or three different areas will probably indicate a different type of rail on the main track from that in a siding. The older type, called the bullhead, has a thickened head on which the wheels run, a thinner section below it, and a foot not quite so thick as the head. It is now to be seen in sidings and on branch lines.

The seating on which the bullhead rail is fixed, called a chair, is a casting fastened to the sleeper either by bolts or heavy screws. The space between the sides of the chair and the rail section is used to take a wooden wedge, called a key. The base of the chair is inclined so as to give an inward cant to the rails and thus help to centre the train wheels on the two rails.

The more modern rail has a wide, flat base spiked direct to the wooden sleeper, or held with a steel bolt to the concrete sleeper, without the need for a chair. An inclined base plate is inserted between the rail and sleeper to provide the same degree of inward cant as with the chair. These modern rails are now universal on main lines.

Rails have become longer and longer as manufacturing and laying techniques have improved. The first cast iron rails were a mere 3 feet long. Modern rails are between 60 and 100 feet in length. They can be joined by fishplates, metal bars bolted at the sides of the rail ends. On modern rails the ends are now welded instead of being bolted together. This provides a smoother run for the train and minimises wear on wheels. Usually the rails from the steelworks are welded into lengths varying from 420 to 1,200 feet at the depot and carried on special trucks to the site of the replacement. These lengths are in turn welded together after they have been laid so as to make a continuous rail of half a mile and more in length.

The problem of expansion of the rail in hot weather, overcome in the case of bolted rails by leaving a small gap between each length, is dealt with in the case of the welded lengths by stressing them to a predetermined degree of tension after laying, and then ensuring that the rail is very firmly fixed to the sleepers and by special expansion joints at the end of each welded length.

Ordinary track, without points, is known as a plain line. In an intricate system such as that in Britain plain lines soon end with points and crossings. The usual ones are single points (a simple junction), single slip (crossing of one line from another), double slip (crossing in both directions), switch diamond (one track crossing another), and catch points (on gradients, and designed to derail any vehicle breaking away and running backwards).

Renewal of the permanent way is, of course, a special operation necessary only at long intervals. It is the responsibility of the Civil Engineering Department and may necessitate renovation of the road's foundations as well as the ballast and the rails and sleepers. The faster and heavier trains of today demand a more solid and better drained foundation. In order to restrict interference with traffic to a minimum much of the work is now mechanised. Trench diggers, to improve drainage, move along the rails and can excavate to a depth of three feet after the ballast has been removed. If the foundation needs no change the ballast is broken up, cleaned and repacked. A mobile ballast cleaner has an endless chain of scoops which passes under the sleepers, the ballast is ejected and screened to remove the dirt and discharged back to the track from a moving belt. The machine moves at about 100 yards per hour while working. After fresh ballast has been added to compensate for the decrease through the screening of dirt, a tamping machine with a battery of rapidly operating hammers packs the ballast under each sleeper, indicators checking the rail level, and controls enabling the operator to vary the pressure of the tamping tools. This machine can pack 700 yards of ballast per hour.

Many kinds of track-laying trains are in use, most working from the adjacent line, though one kind moves along the track being renewed, lifting the section ahead of it, passing it to the rear and lowering the new section into place before it moves on to it to deal with another length of rail.

If renewal of the track is a special job undertaken after long intervals, routine maintenance takes place daily over the 40,000 miles of line operated by British Rail. The men responsible are length gangers. Their expert eyes survey every yard of rail, looking for signs of distortion or other faults. Machines aid the experience of these men. They can electronically detect incipient cracks in the rail, check the degree of cant (tilt) on curves, register any sign of rail distortion, and so on. A typical machine used for this inspection work moves at 18 m.p.h., which is about ten times as fast as was possible when old-time length gangers did the checking, and is more accurate in its findings.

The ceaseless inspection of the railway track, which has made rail travel the safest of any kind of mechanised transport, is a costly business. Apart from the vast sums spent on modernisation, each single track mile of continuous welded rail in Britain costs about £1,000 a year to maintain, while maintenance of bridges, tunnels, embankments, fencing and so on costs a further £800 or so for every route mile.

The work which absorbs this money is basically the result of the daily reports of the length gangers. The men responsible for each section report to an inspector in charge of several sections. He makes an estimate of what needs to be done and forwards his recommendations to his district engineer, who may make a personal inspection, and then puts the work in hand. More important work is reported by the district engineer to the chief civil engineer of the region, and he, after conferences with his experts, draws up a programme of work, taking into consideration the urgency of the different jobs, the availability of machinery, and – most important of all – ways to carry out the work with the minimum disruption of traffic.

There is always controversy between the civil engineers and the traffic men, despite their mutual agreement on striving to provide the best possible service for freight and passengers. The Traffic Department draws up its timetables months in advance and naturally makes the maximum practical use of the rolling stock and the routes on which it runs. Time and speed are their masters, and they dread to learn that the Civil Engineering Department intends to impose speed restrictions, or is even closing a section of line, for essential repair work.

So far as is possible major maintenance work is carried out during the winter, when traffic is lighter than in summer, on Sundays, and at night. Despite all their arguments, both engineers and operators have the common watchword of 'keep the trains moving, and keep them moving on time'.

CHAPTER 2

Signalling

The first railway signal was a human one – an official with police powers appointed to help passengers, prevent theft of goods, and generally control the train service. He told the driver when he could start, mentioned anything of importance about the conditions on the line, and, of course, dealt with any mishap. As trains began to run more frequently he was given more responsibility in seeing that the services kept to time. Gradually he devised a number of positions of his arms and body to indicate whether the line ahead was clear or whether the train must wait. He also stood alongside the line to order a train to stop if a passenger was waiting. With lines being lengthened and intermediate stations constructed, these policemen were soon on duty at each station, gesturing their instructions and becoming the controllers of the train journeys.

Signals by waving arms was not really definite enough, and soon a red flag was being waved to order a stop. At night a lamp with moveable coloured glass plates – white for go ahead, green for caution, and red for stop – was adopted.

When trains began running in both directions on a double track the official could not be in two places at once, and flags or boards were attached to posts to give the signals. By 1837 the invention of the electric telegraph enabled messages to be sent ahead so that signals could be set well in advance of the train's arrival. It was then a normal step to devise a method of operating the signals from a special building by means of wires and levers.

Human errors, causing some collisions and derailments, showed how essential it was to ensure that the signals never provided misleading information, but always reflected the route created by points and switches. The interlocking of signals and points ensured that an accident through the signals indicating one situation and the points set to produce a quite different one became impossible. The first reliable system was invented by John Saxby in 1860.

The original system was entirely mechanical, with locking devices in the signal box on the levers controlling points and signals. Despite all the refinements of today, the interlocking system remains basically the same.

There are two systems in general use today. In one, electric circuits control electro-magnetic locks, eradicating the need for physical strength to operate the old-type mechanical locks so that the massive levers are replaced by tiny ones. The more up-to-date system is completely controlled electrically; push buttons or switches control everything, and if the wrong buttons or switches are used there is no result.

The operation is not unlike that of a telephone. Just as incorrect dialling will not produce a connection or the attempt to use a line in use produces an engaged signal so does the electrical system operate only if the correct routing is selected and the tracks are unoccupied.

Signals and points may be a long distance from the box which controls them. To ensure that they do not fail to obey the orders transmitted to them detectors signal back to the box that the ordered changes have been made. These signals appear in coloured lights on a diagram of the area of the rail system which the box controls. The movement of trains is also shown diagrammatically, with the section of track over which a train is moving operating lights on the diagram. Usually an unilluminated section is an indication of the presence of a train. This provides a greater measure of safety than having the train illuminate the section, which might be misleading should the illuminating lamps fail.

The automatic reporting depends on electrical circuits in the track. Each rail is made into a conductor for a low voltage – and harmless – current flowing between a power source and a relay, the latter being at the end of the section, which is insulated from the adjacent section. When the section is empty current flows along one rail, through the relay, and back along the other rail. The presence of a train's wheels, or indeed any metal object, short-circuits the current, cutting out the relay. The change in current not only provides the information on the signal box diagram, but also operates the locking system and sets the signals just passed by the train at danger.

In urban areas every train runs through a complicated array of points and signals. In modern signal boxes controlling such zones, the signalman needs to press only two master buttons which control the start and the end of the selected route for the train. All points and signals on that route are then set automatically. The apparatus can have a 'memory' so that other routings can be set up and put into operation automatically as soon as conditions permit. If the system is very congested, and trains have to run literally with only a minute or two between them, as on the London Transport system, the 'memory' can look after the running of all trains for hour after hour, receiving its instructions from a punched roll.

The development of automatic apparatus does not mean that the signalman just sits around, checking that his electronic servants are working properly. Passengers tend to believe that everything in a railway timetable is worked out to a precise schedule and this remains unaltered for a whole season. They tend to forget that even in the timetables they consult there is an entirely different schedule for Saturdays and another one for Sundays. They do not pause to think that the freight train they see running through the station may be a special one unique to that day or much longer than usual and therefore running more slowly; or that the long boat train has a schedule dependent on the arrival or sailing time of a liner. Exasperated commuters may be only too well aware that their train is late, but they do not stop to think how just one train running a few minutes late will affect every other train for miles in both directions, not only because of track occupation but because other trains have to connect with it or move over its track for a short distance.

All trains are classified. This means that a Class 1 train (an express passenger train) must be given precedence, if at all feasible, over a Class 2 (local passenger) train, while freight trains, numbered 4 to 9, essential as it may be to keep them moving, are slower and may have to be moved to a side line if they are likely to get in the way of following, faster, trains.

Thus the signalman has to make many quick decisions, or act on urgent instructions, involving constant changes in his operating instructions for the day. A good signalman works almost instinctively, basing his actions on years of experience, in order to ensure that his section is used to its maximum operational efficiency and with the minimum hindrance to every train, whatever its type, he has to handle. The great advantage he has over his colleagues of forty or fifty years ago is that the exhausting physical effort has been obviated and the number of safety devices, eradicating virtually any possibility of error, has increased to ensure that his actions are safe.

The signals he operates convey more vital information to the train drivers than they used to do. Colour light signalling is becoming almost universal. It enables more precise information to be given than with the old semaphore type. The lamps are very powerful, visible for up to a mile in normal conditions. Apart from green and red, the double yellow helps to maintain speed and smooth running in congested areas. A double yellow indicates that the next signal is yellow (not red) so there is no need to slow to a near-stop, but moderate speed can be maintained. Only when a single yellow shows need the driver slow right down, because the next signal is at red.

On sections of plain line a train can operate its own signals, turning the green it has passed to red, the previous one changing from red to single yellow, the one before that from single yellow to double yellow, and the farthest one in the rear from double yellow to green, the sequence continuing as the train passes the green signals ahead.

The driver is further helped by various forms of signal warnings inside the cab, perhaps the most valuable of the devices to ensure close communication between signalman and driver. One device being used on the electrified lines of the Southern Region and on rail systems in some overseas countries reproduces the colour of the signals the train is approaching, and this is combined with automatic braking devices. In Britain another widely used automatic train control system not only gives information about the signals but can take over control of the locomotive. Two magnets are fixed between the rails a few hundred yards in advance of the signal. One magnet is energised only when the signal is green. If this magnet remains dead, because the signal is yellow or red, an instrument in the driver's cab causes a warning horn to sound, and if the driver does not act on it, the brakes are applied after the lapse of a few seconds. A dial also gives a visible warning with yellow marks. The dial returns to black when the train passes over the inductor at the next signal, provided the resetting handle on the indicator has been manipulated to acknowledge the audible warning.

CHAPTER 3

Locomotives

The diesel engine – the 'workhorse' of all modern forms of land transport, both on rail and road – requires far less maintenance than the steam locomotive which it has replaced on the world's railway systems. Its thermal efficiency (the transformation of fuel into energy) is higher than that of any other practical form of engine. It is therefore cheaper to run.

A diesel engine burns fuel oil and air. The oil used has the appearance of petrol, but is not so liable to evaporate or ignite, so fire risks are fewer. The principle on which the engine works is the familiar one in most internal combusion power units of a 4-stroke cycle – induction, compression, expansion, and exhaust.

In the induction cycle the piston is withdrawn from the cylinder, and air sucked in. A diesel engine uses a lot of air – 15 lb of it are needed to burn each 1 lb of fuel.

When the cylinder is filled with air the inlet valve closes as the piston begins to rise, and the air is compressed to about one-sixteenth of its natural volume, to approximately 500 lb per square inch. This pressure raises the temperature to nearly 500° centigrade. At this point fuel oil is being injected in a very fine spray, the quantity controlled by the governor on the engine so that the machine runs at a predetermined speed controlled by the driver. Should he attempt to make the engine run at more than its safe speed a trigger mechanism operates to cut off or reduce the fuel supply.

Because of its high temperature in the cylinder, the injected fuel oil ignites. This is the expansion sequence of the cycle and the source of power. The piston is driven downwards. Just before it reaches the bottom, the exhaust valve in the cylinder head opens, allowing the gases to escape as the piston starts to travel upwards.

The completed cycle occurs several hundred times a minute in each cylinder, the strokes in the different cylinders taking place in a planned sequence. Sometimes the cylinders are in line – as in the type of engine for locomotives of 400-1,000 h.p. Or they can be in a V-form, with pairs of cylinders on each side of the crankshaft. This type is commonly used for locomotives of 1,500 h.p. upwards.

The steam engine had one great advantage over the diesel. It was a self-starting machine, its available power delivered with the first stroke of the piston. Thus it could be linked directly to the driving wheels, and start to haul a train.

But a diesel engine does not develop its full power until it is running at high speed, so the motion must be applied to the driving wheels through a suitable means of transmission to overcome the lack of power when the locomotive starts moving.

The simplest method, as on a petrol-driven car, is a gearbox. It is used on smaller shunting locomotives and some railcars. The power is transmitted through a clutch or hydraulic coupling, the gears being changed by the driver, aided by electrical devices, each gear being used until the maximum speed for that gear is reached; alternatively there can be an automatic gear change as on many modern motor cars.

Hydraulic transmission makes use of the fact that a liquid is virtually incompressible. In diesel locomotives an oil is used. It is contained in a torque converter, the adjustment of the speed of the engine and the running wheels being automatic, the speed of the latter changing according to the resistance produced by the weight of the train, the gradient, and similar factors, without the engine being directly connected by metal rods or gear wheels and thus risking being stalled or strained.

A third and more effective method of overcoming the problem of combining the variations of driving wheel speed with the desirable constant speed of a diesel engine is to make the locomotive a mobile power station, the diesel engine driving a generator to supply current for electric motors mounted on the axles of the locomotive.

Output from the generator can be varied according to the consumption of electricity by the driving motors, it thus being possible to have an infinitely variable speed from the electric motors, ranging from a crawl to the maximum designed speed, without the speed of the diesel engine materially changing, and, of course, with no mechanical link between diesel and driving wheels. Naturally, at slow speeds or while idling, the diesel speed is reduced by the driver, and consequently the armature of the generator revolves more slowly.

A valuable feature of the diesel-electric locomotive is that the electric motors and generator can change their functions – the motors becoming generators and the generator a motor. This reversal is used to start the diesel, the generator turning over the diesel cylinders with power derived from batteries, and the motors are also turned into generators in order to provide braking power.

Diesel-electric locomotives are excellent for long-distance, high-speed work. British engineers led the world in their design, and the 3,300 h.p. Deltics were at the time the most powerful single unit locomotives ever built. They cruised effortlessly at speeds up to 100 m.p.h. Now in both Britain and France there are diesel locomotives of 4,000 h.p.

British Rail now have about 4,100 diesel locomotives of a number of types. The number is likely to be reduced as some of the less powerful types are eliminated, replacing them with a nucleus of types which can undertake most kinds of traction and with components which are in many cases interchangeable. For high-speed passenger trains two loco-units will be included, each of 2,250 h.p. – one at the front of the train and the other at the rear – and capable of speeds up to 125 m.p.h. Among the locomotives for freight haulage there will be a diesel-electric locomotive of 4,500 h.p., by far the most powerful land-based vehicle ever envisaged.

Instead of turning fuel into energy on the rail vehicle, as in the case of the steam- or diesel-engined locomotive, the fuel can be obtained *en route*. This is the method used by an electric-engined locomotive.

An electric locomotive is inexpensive to run and is comparatively simple in construction. The apparatus needed to transform fuel into energy, instead of being part of the locomotive, is in a generating station supplying electricity to other users as well as the railway.

Cheap as electricity is, carrying it to every yard of the track on which an electrically driven train runs is a costly task. It necessitates thousands of track miles of conductor rails or overhead lines. The expenditure of large sums of money on this track equipment is justified only if it is essential to avoid fumes and dirt, as in underground lines, or when the route is a very busy one, such as the suburban networks around large cities, or the main lines serving centres with dense populations and flourishing industries.

Thus the multiple-unit electrically driven trains of the Southern Region serving the southern areas around London could hardly operate by any other source of power so reliably. This network carries the heaviest passenger traffic in the world, most of it concentrated in two periods of two hours each in the morning and evening.

These trains represent the best attainment of power-weight ratio (the amount of energy expended in moving a given weight) achieved in railway engineering. Light, simple motors, two to each motor bogie, and two motor bogies to each group of four passenger cars, can accelerate from rest at the rate of 1 m.p.h. per second, developing 1,000 h.p. in doing so. Electro-pneumatic brakes ensure that deceleration is also rapid, but smooth.

This London suburban network was among the first surface railways to be electrified. As at the time there was no national standard of voltage or type of supply, the engineers chose 750 volts direct current supplied through a conductor rail as their method. Direct current was suitable because d.c. motors were then the most reliable and powerful.

As public electricity supplies were developed, all generating alternating current, it was obvious that the railways would in future take their electricity in this form. It is quite simple to convert alternating current to direct current, and all modern railway electrification projects in Britain are based on using high a.c. voltages up to 25,000 volts fed to the locomotives from overhead lines.

The current is supplied from the National Grid, usually at a very high voltage, and is stepped down at the feeder systems serving the rail system. There is a further stepping down before the current reaches the motors in the locomotive.

The reason for using high voltage a.c. supplies from the power station is that the higher the voltage the less the proportionate loss of power during transmission, and alternating current can be carried through quite thin cables compared with the thick conductor rails needed for direct current at a much lower voltage. There are also safety considerations which favour overhead lines. There is less risk to human beings and animals who may get on the line, and track maintenance is easier.

Inside an express electric locomotive, which is double-ended so that it can be driven in either direction, the two driving compartments are spacious and comfortable. Immediately behind one compartment are the rectifiers and their cooling system; behind the other the exhausters for the brakes and the cooling system for the motors. In the body of the locomotive is the main transformer. The actual motors which drive the wheels are mounted on the bogies.

The reliability of electrical traction, with its economical running at high speed, plus fast acceleration and very powerful braking (permitting high average speeds without omitting stops *en route*), has brought success to British Rail's services on the western route to Scotland. After the line was electrified between London and Crewe, traffic and revenue doubled in three years. When electric locomotives can run the entire 401.4 miles between London and Glasgow (scheduled for 1974), the journey is to take exactly five hours.

This train will thus beat the hitherto unsurpassed record held by a steam locomotive for this run. The Pacific engine *Princess Elizabeth* averaged 70.15 m.p.h. on the non-stop run in November 1936.

The crews who drove the record-breaking expresses of the steam era worked to the limits of human endurance. There can be no denying the strain imposed on the drivers of modern diesel-electric or electric express locomotives, as they control thousands of horse power hauling several hundred tons at $1\frac{1}{2}$ miles per minute, but the physical energy is reduced to a minimum.

When the driver moves the controller to start the train electrical controls operate automatically, with overload switches ensuring that acceleration is not too great. While these devices relieve the driver of activities which might interfere with his concentration on signals and watching his speed so as to maintain his scheduled timing, the complex equipment on these locomotives operates dials and lamps to keep him informed of engine performance and to warn of impending troubles. On some locomotives a needle points to coloured sections recording the amount of current passing into the motors; lamps warn that oil pressure is low, temperature is getting high, driving wheels are slipping, and so on, according to the type of locomotive concerned.

The locomotives which have revolutionised railway transport by replacing the traditional steam engine have capabilities of speeds never attempted as a routine performance on any railway, or, of course, on any public road. In France a series of experiments in 1954-5 marked the real beginning of the new railway era. In the first test, in February 1954, a 4,800 h.p. electric locomotive using 1,500 volts direct current hauled three coaches at 151 m.p.h. on the Dijon–Lyon line. Then, in March 1955, on a specially redesigned track between Bordeaux and Dax, two locomotives, the 106-ton CC7107 and the 81-ton BB9004, hauling three coaches weighing 100 tons, averaged 205.6 m.p.h. over a distance of $1\frac{1}{4}$ miles. Even at this tremendous speed the locomotives were not going all out, but friction between the conductor arms and the overhead power line was so great that the metal began to melt.

Modern locomotives can meet any reasonable challenge for speed. The track is the big problem, and building lines for such high speeds is enormously expensive. In Japan the whole route for the famous 100+ m.p.h. expresses running on the 310-mile trip between Tokyo and Osaka were specially built, with curves practically eliminated. The welded rails are ten miles in length. Every twenty-four hours a test train electronically examines the rails and track base for defects, and every ten days the wheels of the driving wheels of the trains are reground.

1 Switch heaters ensure that points continue to function in conditions of ice and snow

2 A track re-laying machine lowering sleepers into position

3 (*Left*) This portable machine detects by electronic devices invisible flaws and minute cracks in rails

4 (*Below*) A modern rail re-laying machine moving along the track under repair

5 (*Left*) Linesmen servicing the electric motors operating the points

6 (*Below*) A crossover on a double-tracked route

7 The older type of bullhead rail and (8) laying the modern continuous welded rail

9 The two boxes at the side of the track detect overheating in the axle boxes
of any coach or wagon passing them

10 A typical diamond switch near Rugby

11 Powerful cranes speed up repair and renewal work on the track by lifting prefabricated switches and similar pieces of track into position

12 The older type of semaphore signal

13 A modern type 3-aspect colour signal

14 A 4-aspect colour light signal

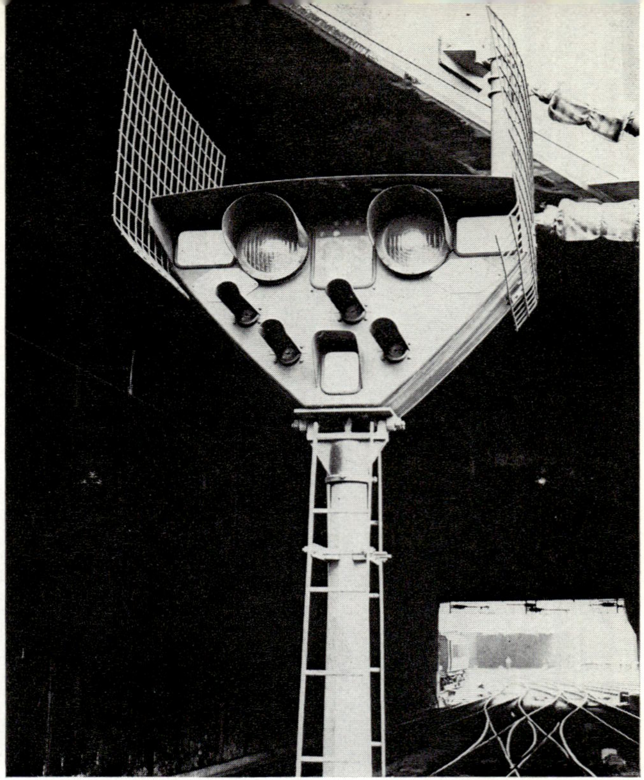

15 A combined single-aspect colour light signal and route indicator

CHAPTER 4

The passenger services

Despite the motor car and the vast network of roads on which it can run the railway remains a vitally important system of mass transport. As an industrial dispute, accident, or other interference with the railway passenger service quickly shows, the mobility in our daily lives which we all expect would quickly become slow or impossible without the railways.

The figures for this ceaseless public service are so large that it is difficult to comprehend them. In Britain the railways provide about 805 million passenger journeys a year, and carry their customers for more than 18,000 million passenger miles. There are some 2,500 stations at which the passengers can board or leave their trains, and close on 5,000 locomotives will take them speedily and safely on their journeys in the 19,000 passenger coaches, each of which travels $2\frac{1}{2}$ million miles in its thirty years of useful life. In these coaches are sufficient seats for nearly $1\frac{1}{2}$ million people to sit down at the same time – more than enough room for every man, woman, and child in Birmingham to travel at the same time.

Yet the earliest railway companies did not consider passengers as a source of revenue: they built their lines only to carry goods. The first man to realise that a railed track offered the chance to carry people quickly, comfortably and cheaply, was a Welshman, Benjamin French. He arranged to run a wagon on a railway built to haul ore and coal between Oystermouth and Swansea. His first horse-drawn passenger wagon rumbled along the track on 25 March 1807, with twelve people on board – the first paying railway passengers in history. This line, incidentally, did not close until 1960, when the last electric vehicle ran along this historic route.

Even when passengers were offered a train service the coaches, merely a copy of the stage coaches running on the turnpikes, were for first class passengers only. Second class passengers had to make do with a truck, open above the waist line, and only in a few instances having an awning to keep out the worst of the rain.

Then in 1844 Parliament passed an Act which forced all railways carrying passengers to run one train a day over every stretch of the line at a speed of not less than 12 m.p.h., with a fare of not more than a penny a mile, and with covered vehicles. These trains were known as Parliamentary Trains. They marked the start of railway transport as a public service as well as a commercial enterprise. This attitude has remained, and many of the passenger services are un-profitable and always will be. Not all of the commuters who pack the trains in and out of London in the rush hours every weekday morning and evening realise that the web of lines, the innumerable stations, and the trains running almost within sight of one another, are not profitable. The formidable task of moving these people during four hours out of the twenty-four, with railway employees, rolling stock and tracks under-utilised in the remaining twenty, is something which can never show a profit if fares are to be kept reasonable and facilities satisfactory.

Despite the closing of branch lines and small stations in recent years the Government always maintains a watchful eye on the social needs of a community, and many such lines and stations remain open to provide a needed service.

Trains are therefore run to cater for the public need, this being matched so far as is possible with the economic factors involved. A high-speed Pullman-type express is a very expensive thing to move across the country. Its eight coaches, carrying 228 passengers in luxury, may weigh up to 400 tons, and to haul that weight at a speed of 90 m.p.h. will need a 100-ton locomotive developing at least 2,200 h.p., with a reserve for gradients, bad climatic conditions, and getting the train moving from a stop.

Whatever the type of train, whether it is an Inter-City express or a branch line railcar, the overriding consideration is the timing of its journey. The advantages of the rail as a smooth running surface and automatic steering device become defects when one train must avoid another. Road vehicles can be steered to the side, can overtake, or can simply reverse out of the way. Unless there are double tracks, loops, or sidings, a railway train must have a reasonably long section of its route entirely to itself.

In order to ensure that every train may run without mishap or delay, time has always been a ruling factor in devising a running schedule. In no other transport system, on land, sea or air, are minutes so highly regarded. A rail journey of several hundred miles is scheduled to the minute for every mile of its length, and more often than not the planned operation is realised in practice. Thus the timetable is the dominant factor in passenger train operation.

The timetables issued to the public, or the tables displayed at railway stations, are very simple compared with the working time-tables used by railwaymen. Those issued for the information of the travelling public list only passenger trains and their times of arrival and departure at stations where they stop, with the minimum of essential additional information such as 'Saturdays only', 'restaurant car', and so on.

The tables compiled in order to run a nation-wide service of trains are necessarily much more complicated. They list every train that is booked for that day – whether it is a famous express, a freight train, or just a locomotive returning to its depot. Further, they show the times each train is scheduled to pass a junction, signal box and control point; the place where the crew may be changed, and which track it will take in stretches of multi-lines. Special details, such as line stops, speed limits, dropping or adding coaches, and so on, are included with every relevant detail.

These tables are the result of research carried out a long time in advance. Train office staff, working in regional headquarters, compile the timetables by working out routes and schedules. Each route is divided into sections, and each section is plotted out on a sheet of graph paper. The distance is marked vertically, with all relevant places in the section – stations, sidings, signal box timing points, etc. – marked. The horizontal line, from left to right, is marked off in time, usually in 30-minute columns.

The journey of a train is then marked in as a graph. In one direction a train's graph will slope from the top left-hand corner of the graph towards the bottom right-hand corner, and a train in the opposite direction from the bottom left-hand corner towards the top right-hand corner. The faster it is to run the more vertical the line will be. Every stop will mean a jerk in the sloping line as for a few minutes the line becomes horizontal.

The simplest way to understand the principle of this timetable graph is to construct one for a journey on foot and by road vehicle on a route with which the reader is familiar.

For example, the route might be from home to the nearest bus stop and thence to a town centre a mile or so away. On a sheet of graph paper every important feature of this route is marked on the left-hand side, vertically – starting with home, one or two places passed on foot, the bus stop, traffic signals and bus stops *en route*, and the town centre destination. These places should be spaced out so that the distances between each of them are in proportion.

Along the top, horizontally, the paper should be marked out in time. A minute for each square will probably be appropriate, and the first time is that at which the journey is started. Now, either by timing oneself or using imagination, a dot is made to denote the time at each place and the dots joined with a line. This will produce a gently sloping line for the slow walk at the outset, a horizontal line during the wait for the bus, and a steeper line for the bus ride, though with a series of short horizontal lines when the bus pauses at traffic lights or other stops. Other lines can be drawn in by plotting the time taken for the same journey by someone walking the whole way, by cycle, and by car. If all start within a few minutes of one another these lines will, of course, cross, as the car overtakes the walker or cyclist.

On the train graph such overtaking is, of course, impossible unless there are double tracks or loops. Sometimes the graph also includes diagrams of the layout of the track along the route so that the planners can immediately see the problem and work out a solution.

The train graph provides an exact picture of how every section of the line is occupied at any given time and at any given point. When extra trains have to be included – freight trains, excursions, boat trains, and so on – the feasible path can be seen in the blank areas of the graph. (*See* plate 40.)

The preliminary work is obviously intricate and demands long experience. It is not, of course, just a question of fitting trains into gaps when a line is unoccupied. First, the needs of the railway's customers must be met. The introduction of faster trains, such as the Inter-City services, the trend towards trains running at regular intervals so that every train on a particular route departs at the same number of minutes past the hour, the scheduling of two trains so that passengers at an interchange station have neither too short nor too long a time to make the connection – all these factors need to be considered. Further, virtually all the trains must run through many other sections, and their problems have to be borne in mind. It is pointless to give an express a clear run through one section if the next section is scheduling a slow-moving freight or stopping passenger train on that track a few minutes ahead of the scheduled time for the faster train.

On top of all these problems is the need to ensure that the utmost use is made of train crews, locomotives, and rolling stock. It is of no use to devise a splendidly clear run for an Inter-City train at some time inconvenient to passengers, nor is it desirable to have a locomotive and rolling stock at some faraway destination at a time when it cannot be used for a return journey for many hours ahead, with the train crew far from their home depot and either unemployed for part of their shift or employed on excess overtime to get them back.

It will now be clear why the timetables which will be new to the public in six or eight months' time already exist on the graphs and are being discussed and modified. Once they are approved more documents will be prepared for the use of railway staffs, locomotive crews' and guards' rosters, station working schedules, carriage rosters, and the working timetables for control offices and signalmen.

A station working table, for example, will list every train the station is due to handle; its time, origin and destination, platform, type of locomotive, and so on. For the department which assembles the trains, every train has to have a carriage roster, showing the type of coach, the order of assembly, and their destinations.

Adherence to all the carefully planned schedules rests ultimately on the efficiency of the train crews. Their rosters are different from those for the locomotives they drive for, obviously, a machine can be worked for many hours on end and its 'off duty days' occur only when it is due for servicing and maintenance, while the crews' shifts are limited by rules and work negotiations.

No driver can work over a route until he is thoroughly familiar with it and has signed a document to that effect. On long distance trains, with crews changed *en route*, this need for experience has to be borne in mind as relief crews are chosen. And, of course, every driver must be experienced on the type of locomotive he is to drive, which is one of the many reasons why standardisation of as few types of locomotive as possible is an advantage.

At every depot a notice board displays details of temporary speed restrictions, repair work, and similar incidents, which will affect train operation. The train crews study this when they report for duty. Having been allocated to a locomotive, they make a routine inspection prior to moving out of the depot.

The guards' rosters are just as detailed. A guard has to be as familiar with the route on which he travels as the engine crew, and the guard is the man with the main responsibility for the safety and efficient running of the train.

The crew of a modern train is chosen with the care akin to that devoted to the selection and training of the crew of an airliner. There are aptitude tests as well as periodic physical check-ups by the Railway Board's medical staff. High speeds, though their attainment involve little physical effort, inevitably create some anxiety in the crew's minds; yet the uneventful passage of the train along a familiar route carries the risk of boredom. Vision, if not perfect, can be blurred by a driver having to stare fixedly ahead, and seeing the sleepers of the track passing below him in a never-ceasing flicker. Despite all the apparatus on train and track to ensure safe operation, the human factor remains vitally important and, indeed, is becoming more so. The modern train driver's job is going to be one of the most fascinating and responsible of any form of public transportation in the new era of Super Trains.

These Super Trains will ensure that the 1970s become a milestone in Britain's railway history. They are scheduled to run at 150 m.p.h. and bring Edinburgh within 3½ hours' travelling time from London. This speed obviously beats any form of road transport, and for distances between 100 and 400 miles can match or improve on air transport, because the train runs direct from the heart of one city to another, while airports, even with helicopter connections, are the cause of heavy time loss despite the 500-plus m.p.h. of the actual flight.

If successful, about a hundred of these trains will be needed to serve the main routes in Britain, the locomotives having either gas turbines or electric motors. The coaches are being designed to include many of the features of an airliner – air conditioning, aircraft-type seating, and sound insulation. In order that the train can maintain high speed on curves the body of the train will tilt, though the passengers will be unaware of it. By suspending the body of a coach the danger of derailment when curves are taken at high speed is avoided. This derailment risk occurs because the wheels 'hunt', moving from side to side. Suspension prevents it.

With these APTs (Advanced Passenger Trains) averaging between 90 and 100 m.p.h. on all routes between London and the big provincial cities, but still using the congested and often sinuous tracks of a more leisurely age, every available device to ensure maximum speed and overall safety will be needed. Modern trains, averaging about 70 m.p.h., need about 5 h.p. for every ton weight of the train in order to maintain their speed. More power can be obtained without a proportionate increase in locomotive weight, but it is more economical and practical to help by reducing weight while using the same power as originally. The APT will weigh about a half of a conventional train carrying the same number of passengers.

Better acceleration and more powerful brakes can save valuable seconds, but the most useful thing is to see that the train has a clear run yet never incurs risks. Signalling systems which really take over from the driver can control the train on every mile of its run. A small computer in the cab digests information transmitted to it by conductors between the rails, giving details of signals, track conditions, and maximum permissible speed. The computer then processes this information and issues data for the driver on a display panel, actually operating the controls if desired, or checking on the driver if he is in charge, and automatically applying the brakes if he exceeds the calculated safe speed. The driver is also in constant two-way contact with the controlling signal box.

CHAPTER 5

Freight trains

In old photographs of railway stations, whether in a large town or serving a rural community on a branch line, a feature of the scene is invariably the adjacent goods yard. Here, long trains of wagons, or just two or three, depending on the station's importance, were shunted about by a fussy little locomotive or even by a horse, and periodically a freight train arrived to which, after more shunting, they were attached and taken away, while other wagons were uncoupled and moved to a siding.

Such sidings have now all but disappeared; hundreds of small goods yards have been closed, their wagons using a yard in the nearest large town, and even here the amount of shunting has been reduced to a minimum.

In the place of the slow, intricate, and expensive methods of moving freight of past years has come the marshalling yard. These are at carefully selected centres fed by all the lines in the area and acting as an exchange place for main lines covering the whole country.

They are the true nerve centres of railway freight transportation. Britain is one of the most densely populated countries in the world; no other nation has such a diverse and widespread pattern of industry. Moving raw materials to the factories and power plants, and carrying the producers' goods to the consumers, is an intricate and ceaseless activity, demanding speed, reliability and cheapness. British Rail needs up to half a million wagons for its work, though the number is decreasing as bigger wagons – carrying up to 100 tons – come into service. Every year the loaded wagons travel more than $1\frac{1}{2}$ thousand million miles, carrying more than 200 million tons of freight.

In all but the most straightforward deliveries the marshalling yards make it possible to operate this vast and intricate transportation service.

The modern marshalling yard is fully automated and operates ceaselessly, day and night. Reception sidings take over the incoming freight train. Its staff have been informed of the wagons in it and their ultimate destination. They prepare a list of the sidings in the yard to which each wagon, or group of wagons, is to be moved according to the destination. This list is called a cut card, the name derived from its purpose in showing how the freight train is to be cut up.

The operator in the control room feeds the information into a control console. This is done by using a card on which the details are punched in a series of holes, by depressing a series of buttons on his console. Electronic apparatus almost instantly sets up the points to run the wagons into their appropriate sidings. Meantime, in the reception siding, the wagons have been uncoupled, there being no movement because the track is on an upward incline and a locomotive at the rear end prevents them rolling downhill. The locomotive then slowly pushes the train until the leading wagon reaches the crown of the hump. The wagon (or group of coupled wagons) at the front begins running down the other side, while the locomotive keeps the remainder, still on the uphill side of the hump, moving very slowly. Once the released wagon has rolled into its siding the points are automatically reset and the locomotive can push the next wagon over the hump and let it roll to its siding, and so on, the locomotive always moving at a speed which ensures that there is the small gap between each group of freely-moving wagons being sorted to allow the points to switch direction.

The marshalling of wagons, it will be realised, depends on their running free at the desired speed. This can, of course, vary according to the type of wagon, its weight, the lubrication of its axles, and so on. The driver of the locomotive has to be skilful in selecting just the right speed to keep his train moving and give the wagons a sufficiently forceful push over the hump. Thereafter the gradient has to be steep enough to ensure that even the lightest and most inefficiently lubricated wagon does not come to rest before it reaches its place in the siding, which may be at a distant part of the yard and at the end of a considerable curve.

With the gradient ensuring adequate speed there has to be a

method of braking to deal with heavy wagons, those moving only a short distance, or those rolling into a siding already almost full. Retarders, which are treads laid alongside each running rail, rise against the flanges of the wagon wheels and grip them with a varying amount of pressure.

The variation in this pressure calls for ingenious devices. One system employs retarders at quite a short distance from the crown of the hump. These electronically make an estimate of the wagon's weight, its length, and its speed. This information goes through a computer which instantly calculates the desirable future speed, and this new information is flashed to the next set of retarders. These apply the degree of braking pressure required to permit the wagon to complete its trip and to stop gently against the wagon already in the siding.

In some marshalling yards television cameras, mounted on pylons in the yard, can be swung round so that the yardmaster can check on every detail of the marshalling over many acres of sidings.

At present in Britain the coupling of the wagons for assembly into groups after they have been distributed has to be carried out by hand. When all wagons have been fitted with continuous vacuum brakes, or with air brakes, as already used on Freightliner and other special freight trains, the possibility of using automatic couplers will abolish even this human activity in a marshalling yard. The difficulty is to devise a reliable coupler in which the connection between each wagon as well as an efficient air-tight link of the vacuum brake pipe are achieved even if the meeting force of the wagons varies. Such automatic couplers are widely used in the United States of America, and satisfactory experiments have been made in Britain.

The complicated operations in a marshalling yard are concerned not only with the destination of the assembled wagons but also with their classification. Class 4 freight trains, for example, are really expresses and are expected to average 50 m.p.h. They carry perishable or urgent merchandise, and because of the speed at which they travel ideally all the wagons must be equipped with continuous braking controlled by the driver. Thus old wagons, probably without vacuum or air brakes and no ball bearings on their axles, cannot be included in a class 4 freight train. This classification of freight trains further complicates the operations in a marshalling yard. Arriving freight trains may have many wagons all scheduled for, say, London. But some wagons may be refrigerated, and loaded with perishable food, while others will have fragile loads. Still others will be loaded with coal for London power stations or heavy machinery due for export through the Port of London. Despite the fact that all are due for despatch on the same route and to destinations in the same locality they have to be allocated to different trains, and therefore to different sidings.

The reception and 'cutting up' of wagons, and their assembly into trains for despatch, is, of course, only one stage of freight handling.

Freight trains involve more complicated working than passenger services. While there are many freighters which run as regularly as a passenger train, the majority vary in timing, route, and size from day to day, according to the needs of industry and the consumer.

The first task is to see that the right type and number of wagons are available in the right place. First thing every morning stations and freight depots prepare schedules reporting the number of wagons received and despatched during the previous twenty-four hours, how many are standing in the sidings (and whether they are full or empty) and how many will be needed for loading that day. The schedule is further broken down with details of the types of wagon, using code names for the sake of brevity. By 10 a.m. this information has been passed from the district control office to the wagon controller for the region.

District control deals with all routine problems. From the scores, perhaps hundreds, of returns, the staff plan movements of empty, unwanted wagons from one depot to another which requires them. Sometimes the day's work is pleasantly simplified by the supply and demand in the district neatly matching, but more usually one district will require a large number of empty wagons, while another one, on the other side of the country, has sidings packed with wagons now empty and unrequired. Why this imbalance occurs is easy to understand. A district with coal mines constantly despatches train-loads of coal to another district with a large power station or a town with a dense population. The latter district produces nothing which needs to be carried away in coal wagons after they have been emptied. Similarly, the industrial north may send huge quantities of merchandise to the ports for export. The goods being imported at those coastal districts are usually of a different kind, needing other types of wagon, and in any event need to be distributed to other regions.

When district control is unable to meet its own wagon requirements, regional control takes over. The staff study the returns for the districts in that region, and order the movement of wagons to meet district needs, devising schemes to ensure a minimum of journeys with empty wagons.

When regional control cannot solve the problem central control in London can order wagons to be moved from one region to another. Frequently central control is presented with the problem of two regions demanding wagons, and the decision has to be made as to which gets priority for all of them or whether each must get a share and, if so, in what proportion.

This planned movement, inevitably involving trains of empty wagons which may, if the number is large, be moved specially, or if not many are involved, may be added to an already scheduled freight train, is merely the preliminary of the work. The merchandise has to be loaded, wagons assembled, a locomotive allocated, and the train taken to the marshalling yard. Both the incoming trains and the outgoing ones must be fitted into the timetable without interfering with the passenger services running on the same routes.

Even if the freight train is a booked one – running to a regular schedule and on a regular route – its size may vary greatly. Control has to assess whether a small load should be added to another train or whether an abnormally large load will mean running an extra train.

The control rooms, in which the staff work shifts round the clock, plan the train movements and keep a constant check that they are running smoothly. The first task is to work out timing, taking into account the speed of the freight train, and the need not to delay passenger services. This means ensuring that either the train finds a time gap on the route or else that there are sidings, loops or alternative routes which the freight train can use in order to keep out of the way without being seriously delayed. That done, checks must be made that there are an available locomotive of adequate power and a train crew whose hours of work and location will permit them to drive it. Finally, the operation must not be wasteful. Locomotive and crew must not have to travel a long distance before working the train or end up at a station from which they must return with no train to work.

The actual movement of every freight train is followed by the control centre in each district and region from reports which come in from signalmen and other control offices along the route. Inevitably there are problems to solve: fog and other climatic upsets, lines under repair, delays through mechanical troubles, changes in schedule because a train with greater priority is running late, or a driver unexpectedly fails to report for duty. Then quick decisions have to be made about revisions of the schedules. It is never a question of just getting the train out of the way. It may have perishable goods like fruit, fish, or meat. The freight may be carrying goods getting priority as urgent exports for loading on an ocean-going cargo liner. In every case every customer with merchandise on every train expects fast, reliable service of the promised standard. To meet the demands is a challenge. That it is nearly always successfully met is proof of the efficiency and resourcefulness of the men who move tens of thousands of wagons every twenty-four hours as if they were players of a game of unbelievably complicated chess.

A modern development in freight delivery is concerned with loads which travel on the same route, are of roughly the same bulk, and are needed at regular intervals – a clockwork regularity now being met by what is known as a merry-go-round train. It is used principally for carrying coal from pit head to electricity generating station. The train has a specially modified locomotive hauling high-capacity coal wagons running as a complete unit, loaded with up to 1,200 tons of coal. At the coal mine the wagons move at about 15 feet per minute, while mechanical loaders deposit just the correct amount of coal into each wagon. With all wagons full, the locomotive, geared to move at its very low speed in the loading bay, accelerates to normal speed to its destination, where once again the speed drops to a crawl while each wagon's load is automatically discharged into hoppers feeding the power station furnaces. Thus in its working hours, the merry-go-round freight train never completely stops.

Finally, a vitally important freight service which benefits everyone in the country almost every morning. This is the transport and distribution of the mails. Night after night hundreds of millions of letters and packets are conveyed by rail to ensure that, for the first class rates, mail is delivered from any place in the country to the addressee in twenty-four hours.

Although mail is technically freight, it is handled in a special category, and, except for parcels in periods of very heavy traffic, on passenger trains. Many expresses have mail coaches attached to the passenger rolling stock. The basis of the rapid transport of mails is however, the four specials which run every night. They are the Travelling Post Offices, or T.P.O.s.

The Great Western Down and the Great Western Up run between London and Penzance, a distance of 305 miles. The Up Special and the Down Special are on the run from London to Glasgow and Aberdeen, a distance of 524 miles. It was the Up Special which was held up near the end of its journey in the infamous Mail Train Robbery in 1963. The fact that the T.P.O.s always have a large amount of registered mail aboard is one reason why no passenger coaches are included in these trains, and no passengers are ever allowed to travel in the special coaches. Nor are any details of the trains included in public timetables, though for the signalling staff the schedules are very important, for, of all trains, the T.P.O.s must have an unhindered run, often exceeding 80 m.p.h.

The coaches, painted in blue and grey, and bearing the Royal Insignia with the words 'Royal Mail', are specially built to Post Office requirements. There are both stowage and sorting coaches, and in normal conditions each train consists of seven sorting coaches and five stowage coaches.

The staff begin work at least an hour before the train leaves. Some of the mailbags delivered by vans and the Post Office London underground railway will contain mail already sorted into towns or regions. These may be left untouched in the stowage vans, stocked in a definite order so that they can be unloaded easily at the required destinations.

Unsorted mail is dealt with by the sorters at lightning speed, for the first drop will come within half an hour or so after the train's departure. The sorted mail has to be bundled, put in a bag, and sealed. If it is to be dropped without the train stopping the mail goes into a heavy leather pouch strong enough to withstand impact as it leaves a train rushing at more than 60 m.p.h.

The mail drop is handled by men with long experience of the line. In pitch darkness they sense, by the sound of the wheels passing over a bridge or a series of points, exactly the train's position. These sounds are more reliable than the timing of the train, however precise that may be. For a drop seconds are vital; minutes hardly count.

The sliding door of the mail coach is pushed back, and the operator prepares to manipulate the supporting arms from which the mail pouch is suspended. At the drop point a heavy rope net is suspended at the side of the track, with a wire cable stretched across a hinged iron frame. As the train passes the drop point, the straps holding the pouch, by this time swung out on the supporting arms, hit the wire cable. The bag is released and drops into the rope net.

Mail is picked up by means of a strong net swung out from the train. This net is at the same height as the leather mail pouch, which is suspended from a metal post. The pouch is hurled by the force of impact through the open door of the mail coach. This procedure can be dangerous, and just before mail is due to be picked up a bell rings to ensure that the train staff keep clear.

The T.P.O.s make a series of stops during their nightly runs. At junctions coaches previously hauled by a passenger train will be attached and a stowage coach with sorted mail detached. In large towns more stowage coaches will be detached or added. Locomotives are ready to haul detached sections to regions off the main route of the T.P.O.

Some of the staff alight at these towns, returning to their base on the T.P.O. travelling in the opposite direction, or in the case of those who may work from London as far as Carlisle, there are eighteen hours or so off duty until they join the Up Special on the following night.

The work of the men on the T.P.O.s is probably as onerous as any in the railway or Post Office services. Every year they sort about 600 million letters and packets, all of them dealt with while these four Travelling Post Offices roar over some 1,700 miles of track in order that our mail shall be delivered at breakfast time.

A view of part of the control panel at Old Oak Common, near
Paddington

17 A general view of the signal box at Euston

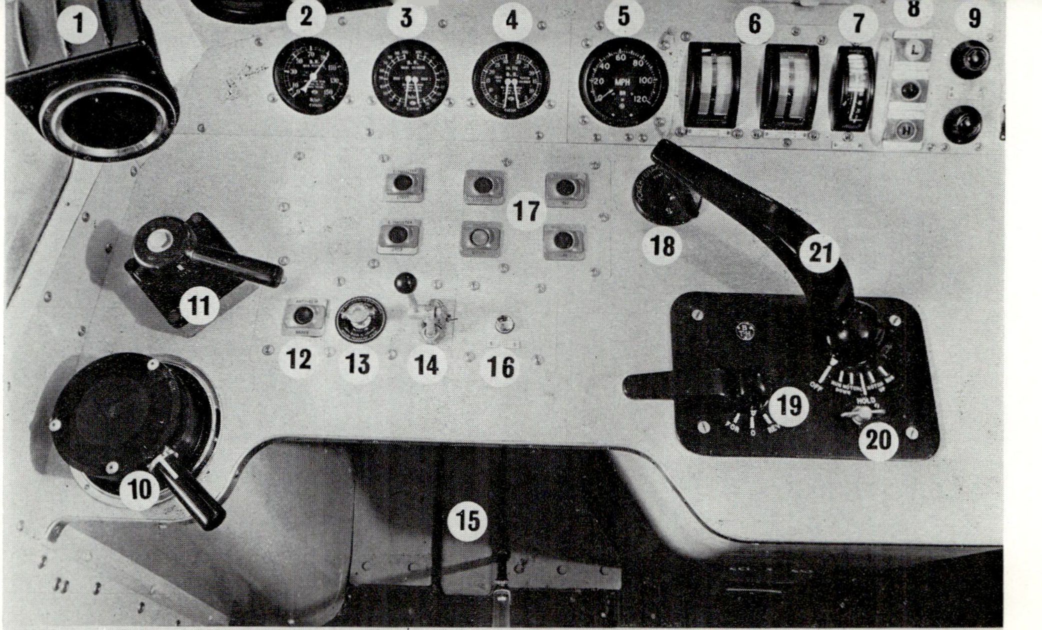

18 The controls and instruments in the cab of an electric locomotive

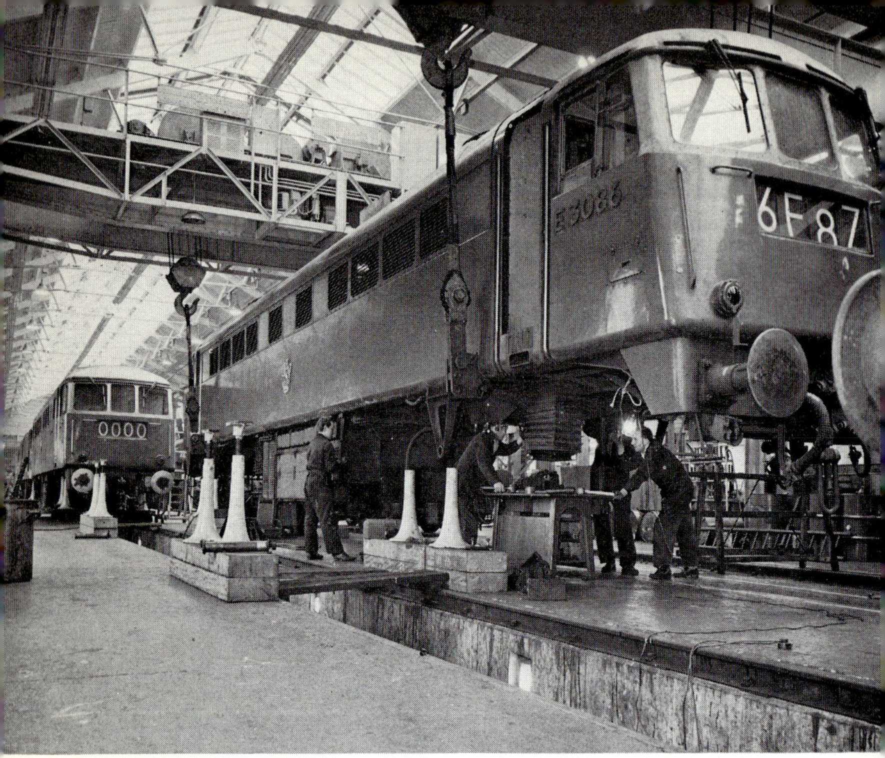

19 Part of the maintenance and repair shops at Crewe

20 An 86 Class electric locomotive

21 A Deltic Class locomotive hauling a Newcastle–King's Cross express

22 Probably the most famous train in the world: the Flying Scotsman, here seen pulling out of Waverley station, Edinburgh

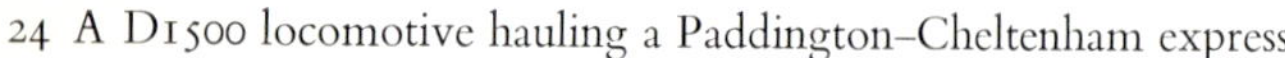

23 Luxury in modern train travel: the Blue Pullman at speed through
Sonning cutting, Berkshire

24 A D1500 locomotive hauling a Paddington–Cheltenham express

25 Another famous express: the Royal Scot, here seen cruising through a crossover at Crewe. Note that the train is double-headed

26 Multiple-unit trains provide a fast, useful service for medium distance routes

27 An Inter-City express near Leighton Buzzard. It covers the $193\frac{3}{4}$ miles between Liverpool and London in 168 minutes – an average of nearly 69 m.p.h.

28 Third rail electrification systems are used in urban areas of dense traffic

CHAPTER 6
Types of railway

So far there has been no mention of those vitally important railways which are the arteries of many of the world's biggest cities – the underground railways networks. Basically, of course, they differ little from surface railways in actual operation. Many such underground lines run only a few feet below the surface, and were constructed on the 'cut and cover' system, each stretch of the route being excavated from the surface and then covered over. This system was used for the Metropolitan and District lines in London.

The invention of the Greathead shield by a South African, James Greathead, made possible the deep tunnelling through London's clay for the world's greatest underground railway system. This shield consists of a ring of steel which is forced forward by hydraulic rams, the piston heads driving forward from the lining of the section of tunnel just excavated. If the terrain is suitable, power-driven knives cut into the earth. The removed material is then carried away on conveyors. The shield can cut about two feet of tunnel at a time before being moved forward. Gravel, sand, and water present real difficulties. Sometimes the area to be excavated is frozen to solidity, or the surrounding area is injected with cement, chemical grouts, and special plastics.

All underground railway systems are built to provide a fast and frequent service, and this means that they have been the leaders in developing high performance multi-unit trains and highly efficient foolproof signalling systems.

Operational techniques reached a new standard with the opening of the Victoria line in London in 1969. The trains on this line are controlled entirely by coded track circuits, though each train carries a driver, partly to reassure a public not yet accustomed to robot trains and partly to take action in the remote chance of a fault. But the driver is really the guard, for his main job is to operate the doors at each station; he need not actually drive the train.

Each train on the Victoria line has electronic apparatus which records instructions and learns whether the track ahead is clear, the information coming from equipment at the side of the track. The train does not merely obey by starting or stopping; it is also told when to coast without power, when to increase speed, and when to apply the brakes. On the Victoria line the time gap between trains can be cut to under 90 seconds without any danger, and trains can thus operate at great speed and frequency. The regular bursts of 50 m.p.h. are by far the fastest times for any underground train in the world.

Driverless trains will undoubtedly be commonplace in the future, and have, indeed, been a reality for a long time past. The Post Office tube running under London, carrying letters and parcels between the main sorting offices, on a double track of 2-foot gauge, has been entirely automated since it was opened in 1927. These unmanned trains average 35 m.p.h. between stations.

There is not much of an advantage in providing fast and frequent transport if passengers are delayed at the start and end of their journey. This is a prevalent complaint about air travel. While people travelling many hundreds of miles may put up with a delay of an hour at the airport, passengers on tube railways, expecting to complete their journey in a matter of minutes, will not accept hold-ups at station entrances and exits. Here automation has come to the rescue, and on the stations serving the Victoria line machines 'process' passengers.

Automatic fare collection is the job of the barrier gates. The ticket carries an invisible code which records the date, the fare paid, and the station at which it was bought. At the passenger's destination the machine, when presented with the ticket, registers the details and if all is in order, it accepts the ticket and allows the barrier to open. If the details suggest the ticket is invalid the machine will reject the ticket and the barrier remains closed. Each barrier can handle up to forty-five passengers a minute (far higher than necessary on an average day) so that with an adequate number of barriers passengers can be handled as fast as the trains can carry them. And on London's tubes these numbers are very great. They have carried more then two million passengers in one day.

Just as railways have gone below the earth's surface so have they conquered the mountains wherever there is some advantage in providing a means of transport to the summits. Any incline steeper than 1 in 36 creates problems of adhesion for conventional locomotives and rails. The difficulty on most mountain railways is overcome by the rack-and-pinion system. Usually there are two racks, laid alongside the running rails, so placed that the teeth of one rack correspond with the notches on the other. Two toothed pinions on the locomotive engage with these racks, the staggering of the teeth ensuring that the grip is secure and regular.

It is strange to realise that many of the pioneer railway engineers refused to believe that there could be sufficient adhesion between a smooth wheel and a smooth rail to produce motion without a large amount of slipping. This was the reason why the Leeds engineer, John Blenkinsop, who was a forerunner of Stephenson in developing a steam locomotive, went to the expense and trouble of laying down a test track and building an engine with rack and pinion. The system did, in fact, work well, and in 1812 his locomotive travelled $1\frac{1}{2}$ miles in twenty-three minutes, 'without', as Blenkinsop proudly reported, 'the slightest accident'.

Efficient rack-and-pinion railways have been running for more than a century. One of the most famous is the Rigi line beside Lake Lucerne in Switzerland. It rises more than 5,000 feet in its three-mile length, averaging a 1 in 3 gradient. On the other side of the lake, on Mount Pilatus, is another famous rack-and-pinion railway, with an even steeper track. On its 6,500-feet climb some stretches have a gradient of nearly 1 in 2. Britain's famous rack railway to the summit of Snowdon climbs 3,500 feet. It is a narrow gauge line – 2 feet $7\frac{1}{2}$ inches.

Special locomotives are needed for these rack railways. They usually have separate steam cylinders or electric motors for the pinion wheel and for the ordinary adhesion wheels.

Cable railways are another idea originating from the earliest years of rail transport. The stationary steam engine was, of course, in widespread use long before the steam locomotive was perfected.

The low-pressure, condensing type of steam engine developed by James Watt was much too large and heavy to be mounted on wheels and made mobile. For this reason the early engineers began to experiment with engines at the end of the line hauling wagons by a long rope.

A number of such rope-and-engine lines were built. The famous incline of Camden Bank, outside Euston station in London, was originally such a line. From 1837 to 1844 trains were hauled up the gradient by a stationary engine and ran down it by gravity. For more than a century this incline meant that heavy trains had to be aided by a second locomotive pushing at the rear.

The most efficient of these railways ran from Fenchurch Street to Blackwall in the east London area. For the first eight years of the railway's existence, after 1841, two stationary engines provided the motive power, trains running in both directions, hauled by ropes which were $3\frac{1}{2}$ miles in length. Express trains covered the distance in five minutes, and the ordinary service took eight minutes – far quicker than it is possible to make this journey either by road or rail today.

There were inevitable difficulties with the ropes because the hemp quickly frayed, and when steel cables were tried they tended to kink or get twisted.

If these problems had been overcome at the outset there might have been many more cable railways. It was to settle the controversy between the supporters of the new-fangled locomotives and the champions of rope-and-engine tracks that the historic Rainhill trials were held in 1829, resulting in the complete triumph for Stephenson's *Rocket*.

Motion on mountain cable railways is achieved in a number of ways. Hydraulic power is employed by pumping water into the car at the summit so that it weighs more than the car at the base; electric power is nowadays in general use to drive the cable drum at the summit, the extra energy compensating for the inertia which would otherwise keep the two cars of almost equal weight motion-less.

A famous cable railway is that which climbs to one of the summits of the Wetterhorn in the Bernese Oberland in Switzerland. At places this line is at a gradient of 1 in 1¼. There are double cables in each direction, one above the other, to minimise swaying. Perhaps more remarkable is the cable railway on the Kohler mountain in the Tyrol. The cables are one mile long. The cars move at 5 m.p.h.

There have been other attempts to make the motive power a permanent part of the track, the cars being unpowered vehicles. There are advantages in such a system for short routes with a high traffic density, and the notable one is economy of operation.

A novel one was built at Wembley, Middlesex, for the exhibition held there in 1924. It was an overhead non-stop railway running on a continuous track with numerous stations. Fixed beside the rails, and below the surface, was a continuously rotating spiral of steel, powered at intervals by motors. At the stations the spirals were very close together, gradually widening beyond them. The cars were attached to the spiral by a hollow link. Consequently, the corkscrew effect moved a car very slowly indeed when the car passed a station, and more quickly as each spiral widened to about 2½ feet. The defects were that a motor breakdown brought every car to a standstill, overall speed was very low, and the public of those days were unwilling to board or leave a moving car, even though the motion was for some seconds a very slow crawl.

Another idea is the pneumatic railway. Pneumatic tubes, in which small objects such as documents, telegrams, and packets are driven along by suction or compressed air, have long been the cheapest and quickest means of carrying such articles over quite long distances. A velocity of 30–40 feet per second (about 20–25 m.p.h.) is usual in order to minimise friction and damage in these pneumatic carriers, but there would be no technical problem in increasing the pressure for much higher speeds.

The latent power in either compressing air or sucking it out to create a vacuum intrigued the early railway engineers. As long ago as 1847 there were two lines using a pneumatic system, one running between Forest Hill and West Croydon and the other between Newton Abbot and Exeter. The train was attached by a rod to a piston which was enclosed in a pipe running between the rails, a close-fitting slot at the top allowing the connecting rod to pass from piston to the underside of the train. A steam engine at the far end then pumped out the air and the piston was sucked along, taking the train with it. The speed attained was far in excess of anything ever experienced by a human being before – claimed to be 75 m.p.h. for short distances and confirmed in 1847 at 60 m.p.h. Unfortunately these pioneers had only leather to seal the slot in the pipe. It leaked badly, and was quickly spoiled by weather conditions and gnawing animals.

The success of the Newton Abbot–Exeter pneumatic railway resulted in the famous railway engineer Isambard Brunel planning this method of propulsion for a new track between Newton Abbot and Totnes. Accordingly he did not worry overmuch about gradients, there being no problem of wheel adhesion and the power being ample to keep the trains running at a good speed. Generations of locomotive drivers have since regarded this stretch of line as one of the most formidable in Britain. Gradients vary from 1 in 57 to 1 in 36 and there are many curves on the 4-mile stretch. No engineer, least of all Brunel, would have built such a difficult line for conventional working by locomotives – and its existence is visible proof of the usefulness of the vacuum as a means of propulsion.

CHAPTER 7

Railways of the future

Look at almost any artist's impression of the town of tomorrow and there is bound to be a futuristic railcar gliding quickly above the multi-level streets. It is running on a monorail. The idea is attractive because a monorail can serve the heart of the city and can still be kept clear of the streets. The construction of the track is much cheaper and simpler than burying the conventional type of railway below the surface.

Civil engineers, already starting construction of tomorrow's cities, have remained unenthusiastic about the overhead monorail. Manchester, San Francisco, and Rotterdam are among the cities which have thought about monorails and eventually rejected them in favour of rail systems of the conventional kind.

But a few short monorails have proved quite successful and there can be little doubt that they will become part of tomorrow's railway services, catering for special needs, such as transit to and from airports or across difficult terrain in overseas countries (a monorail needs very little foundation for the track).

One successful system uses a rail shaped like the letter A. The coaches have running wheels in the centre and projecting into the underside of the coach, in which the seats are set back to back against the wheel shield. Small, free-running wheels at the base of the coach help to balance the train.

Another system, which was a true monorail, employed two gyroscopes revolving vertically in opposite directions, thus creating a balance as occurs when a bicycle is propelled. The gyroscopes were mounted on special ball bearings so that they kept revolving for a considerable time even if the motive power was cut off, thus preventing the train from toppling over. The defect of this system was that the gyroscopes were heavy and bulky, and took up almost as much room as the space for profitable loads of freight or passengers. But with lighter alloys, and more compact motors, the gyro-scope monorail might be revived for tomorrow's high-speed 'feeder' services.

The problem of maintaining the balance of a train above a monorail can be solved by suspending the coaches below it instead. By constructing a steel or reinforced concrete girder, square shaped and hollow, the twin running wheels can use a track along the inside lower edges of the girder, with suspension bars hanging down through the bottom aperture of the girder to which the coach is fixed. The girder can be used as a conductor for an electrically powered train, the quietest type available, and noise would be further reduced by fitting the running wheels with rubber tyres. The reduction in friction between wheels and running track, and the fact that careful design can start a tendency for the coach to lift at speed, thus reducing the actual weight resting on the girder, means that such a monorail system could reach high speeds at a comparatively small expenditure of power.

An even simpler method of using a single rail, this time merely as a guide, is the subject of experiment. The coach uses the principle of the hovercraft with a cushion of air between the base of the coach and the track surface. The hovercraft is not easy to steer as a free-moving land vehicle. By having a guide rail, either a slotted one rather like that used for model racing cars, or a moulded one fitting quite closely to the concave underside of the coach, this disadvantage can be largely eradicated. Again, the problem of noise might well make such a hovercraft train unsuitable for use in densely populated areas, but the idea has great possibilities for use in undeveloped countries. The guide rail would be infinitely cheaper and quicker to construct than the simplest road, and there would be no need to construct river bridges. The craft would simply leave the guide rail, cruise just above the water, and pick up the guide rail on the other side.

Completely new versions of a rail system are, in practical terms, of interest only in the case of the comparatively few projects for new routes. As there are several million miles of the conventional two-rail track in the world the important future developments will be to build more efficient locomotives to run on those tracks.

New forms of motive power for railed vehicles have been the subject of many experiments. Jet and rocket propulsion sounds feasible enough, but a number of major objections make it unlikely that they will ever be used except on test tracks. One snag is noise, and as railways exist to serve densely populated areas this could well be a reason for legal prohibition of their use. The high speeds which such motors would permit could not be exploited except on special tracks, and the overwhelming advantage of railed transport – the movement of very heavy weights – would be largely unused. There is little benefit to the community in providing vehicles accommodating no more passengers than an aircraft or road coach.

None of these objections apply to the gas turbine, except, perhaps, some noise problems, now being successfully tackled. Many engineers believe that gas turbine locomotives will be in universal use before the next century on long distance routes with few stops and heavy loads. It will be used on Britain's Advanced Passenger Train.

Gas turbines are comparatively simple in construction and the entire unit is very compact and light for its power. The turbine runs most efficiently at high speeds – 10,000–15,000 revolutions per minute – so there has to be a great reduction by gearing between engine and driving wheels.

The gas turbine has, in fact, been in use for some time. The Russian State Railways use them for hauling heavy freight trains on routes which often mean a journey of a thousand miles. In America they are used to haul iron ore and coal trains on runs of 500 miles and more. These American freight trains are far heavier than anything known in Britain. A rolling weight of 13,000 tons – the legal weight permitted – is not unusual.

Gas turbines on these freight locomotives are different from the small models being developed for high-speed rail cars or small multi-units. Based on the design for aircraft engines, they take up no more room than a low-powered diesel engine and can therefore be slung beneath the coach body.

A very promising type of engine, now the subject of experiments in Holland, Germany, Sweden, and the United States, is driven by hot air. The principle is simple, and was in fact used in a pumping engine made by a Scotsman, Robert Stirling, back in 1816, and then almost forgotten except as a museum curiosity. Air expands under heat in a cylinder, drives a piston, escapes to a cooling chamber, and is then reheated in the cylinder, the cycle being repeated over and over again. There is no explosion and no exhaust gas, so a locomotive with a hot air engine would be quiet and clean. In the modern experimental engines helium is used instead of air. The gas is heated to more than 700° centigrade and has by then expanded to more than a hundred times the pressure of the atmosphere. Any kind of fuel can be used to heat the helium, including electricity or radio-active materials.

Another promising development is the linear electric motor, which appears to be ideal for railway use. When the properties of electricity were first discovered, the object of the early inventors was to construct a device in which the magnetic field created a turning motion. Thus virtually all electric motors turn a wheel. If the circular stator, the stationary part of an electric motor, is opened out and extended for the length of the wiring, the field of current will then travel along it instead of round and round it. Thus by putting the rotor, the rotating part of an ordinary electric motor, in a flat plane above the stator it will follow the field of current along the stator, producing movement without any physical contact between stator and rotor.

For use on a railway, the conductor rail becomes in effect a stator many miles in length, and the rotor, in the train, will follow the field of the current until it reaches the end (or the current is switched off). The roles of stator and rotor can easily be exchanged, with the stator mobile and the rotor fixed. Such linear motors, still in the experimental stage, would cut out much of the friction that exists in using conventional electric motors for rail propulsion. The possible speed is far greater than would ever be practical for land-borne vehicles.

Yet another exciting development of the electrically-powered rail vehicle (though it could equally be driven by a jet engine) is the magnetic train, a model of which was shown at the Japanese exhibition Expo 70 and, it is hoped, will be in routine operation on the Tokyo–Osaka line in the 1980s.

The basis of this vehicle's operation is magnetism. In order to provide the powerful forces needed to lift the vehicle just clear of the track the magnets are enclosed in a jacket of liquid helium which produces a cold so intense that it approaches absolute zero. In this cold internal resistance to electrical currents almost disappears, and the tiniest electrical pulse will keep current flowing indefinitely. Thus comparatively little power is needed to create enormously strong magnetic fields.

At rest and at low speed the train rests on its wheels. As speed increases the helium-enclosed magnets on the underside cause current to flow in the rails which are merely strips of metal. The current in the rails builds up its own magnetic fields, and these are repelled by the magnets on the train, the result being that the train is lifted off the ground. On curves the train will obviously begin to slither sideways in order to continue in a straight line. But the magnetic forces on the inner side of the curve become stronger, pulling the train back to the desired path.

With the train hovering perhaps six inches above the track friction is of course non-existent and tremendous speeds are theoretically possible. The Japanese envisage their magnetic express of the 1980s completing the 310-mile journey between Tokyo and Osaka in a little over one hour.

Such speedy service between two large towns may justify the enormous costs of building the train and providing the track. There will be many other routes in all industrialised countries where such expenditure is justified, but for most of the world's railways such super trains are likely to be rarities. Railways will continue, as always, to provide the best possible service for the greatest number of people, and not something unique for the fortunate few.

Railway careers

The foregoing pages will have shown how varied is the work needed to keep the trains running and to provide the services which the railway's customers expect. It would, indeed, be difficult to mention any kind of job which is not available within the railway service. Rail has its own ships and hotels, policemen and doctors, architects and lawyers, artists and writers, quite apart from the more obvious personnel directly connected with the passenger and freight trains and the lines and stations which they use. Not the least attractive feature is that, whatever the job, the employee becomes a member of an organisation proud of its traditions and team spirit. Railwaymen are like sailors: they feel they belong to a special world.

At the very top of a railway organisation there has to be one man. In Britain he is Chairman of the British Railways Board. Next to him is the Deputy Chairman who is also known as the Chief Executive, and he heads a management group composed of high executives controlling all the railway operations – passenger, freight, finance, staff, and so on – and the general managers of each region of the railway system.

A railway has two main tasks. The first is to provide and maintain the equipment to run the nation's greatest individual transportation service moving 200 million tons of goods and capable of making 805 million passenger journeys every year; this work comes basically under the heading of engineering. The second is the organisation and operation of the railway services, which are the functions of the traffic departments.

Under the first heading the great changes now occurring in railway services have created a host of interesting problems, with as interesting jobs to solve them. Engineering work falls into four main categories.

The first is civil engineering, concerned with the permanent way, bridges, tunnels, stations, marshalling yards, and all the other numerous constructions needed to maintain a railway service.

The second, mechanical and electrical engineering, deals with all the mobile items of railway working – locomotives, multi-unit trains, carriages, and wagons – together with the means of supplying the power: the cables, conductor rails or overhead wires, transformer stations, fuel supply points, and so on. In addition, this section designs and maintains all the ancillary equipment needed to service rolling stock, freight, and passengers: such as cranes, lifting tackle, track laying equipment, machine tools, lifts, and freight handling machinery. There are fifteen railway workshops controlled by a subsidiary company. They are distributed around Britain to deal with the work of the mechanical and electrical engineering department, manufacturing as well as servicing and repairing rolling stock.

Signalling and telecommunications engineering is the third department. This is possibly the most exciting and progressive of all railway engineering, making experiments to meet the demands of the 100–150 m.p.h. trains of tomorrow. The staff does not deal merely with signalling. It is responsible for public-address systems on stations, closed-circuit television in marshalling yards and large stations, teleprinter networks, and the railways' own telephone and radio systems.

Supporting these departments, both inaugurating new ideas and tackling problems their colleagues report, is the Research Department. Its centre is at Derby, and there are six other laboratories in other towns. This department was responsible for the design and development of the Advanced Passenger Train. The term 'research' covers virtually every form of modern scientific investigation: medical (as regards passenger comfort and locomotive crews' health), metallurgy, computers, electronics and electricity, chemistry, dynamics.

The second main heading – traffic – naturally involves close liaison with the engineering departments. In effect traffic operation is akin to production; the moving vehicles are the 'products' of the railway 'factory'. The 'products' must be useful, reliable, and available at an attractive price. Thus traffic first of all concerns itself with train running, signalling, the movement and control of rolling stock, the engagement, training, and welfare of train crews, the organisation of stations and freight depots.

In addition there is the organisation of the railways' ancillary transport services: road vehicles and shipping, with the garages and ports they use, and the provision of these services has to be costed to ascertain the prices at which they can be profitably provided.

The 'railway product' must be sold to the customer. This involves market research, salesmanship, and advertising.

Now as to the opportunities for jobs:

On the engineering side British Rail annually offers scholarships to boys leaving school who plan to study for an honours degree in civil, mechanical, electrical, or electronic engineering. Each scholarship is worth about £600 a year, and essential university fees and the cost of textbooks, drawing instruments, and so on, are met. These grants are, of course, in addition to whatever financial assistance the student may be eligible to obtain from his local authority.

The scholarship scheme is based on a 1–3–1 course: one year of practical training on the railway, three years (and sometimes four) at a university, and a further year of practical training after graduation. In this last year a salary of about £1,200 a year is paid, and on completion of the course a permanent appointment is made with a starting salary of about £1,500 a year.

Another degree course is designed to help boys who want to obtain an engineering degree at a technological university, polytechnic, or regional college, where 'thin sandwich' courses are available. These courses last four to five years and consist of alternate periods of study and practical work on the railway system. From the outset the student becomes a staff member and is paid a salary, whether studying or engaged on practical work.

Men who are graduating from a university, and have, or can expect, a good honours degree usually get two years' training, starting at about £1,200 a year plus allowances. There are posts in civil engineering, mechanical and electrical engineering, signalling and telecommunications, and in research.

On the traffic and operational side opportunities are even more numerous and varied, with training at the outset designed, in some instances, to help the young employee to select the type of work for which he is best suited after he has had some experience. School leavers, with the appropriate passes, can be selected to join a student-ship scheme with two years of varied training, including facilities to study for graduateship of the Institute of Transport. The usual starting age is seventeen, with a salary of about £700, automatically increasing on each subsequent birthday.

Other special training schemes are provided in finance and accountancy (for both young men and women), estate management (British Rail is one of the largest landowners in the country), and corporate planning (which covers the economic side of railway operation).

All school careers teachers have full details of the special opportunities for progressive jobs on the railways, and at all universities there is either a British Rail contact officer or the University Appointments Board has facilities to arrange an interview with a senior railway executive.

Full details of the training schemes and the way to apply can be obtained from the British Railways Board, 222 Marylebone Road, London NW1, or from the Assistant General Manager (Staff) in the applicant's own area of British Rail. The addresses are:

Eastern Region: Headquarters Offices, York.
London Midland: Euston House, Eversholt Street,
    London NW1.
Scottish: Buchanan House, 58 Port Dundas Road,
    Glasgow C4.
Southern: Waterloo Station, London SE1.
Western: Paddington Station, London W2.

29 A buffet car providing sandwiches and drinks

30 Modern passenger coaches are spacious and luxurious, with movable tables and aircraft-type seats. This is a second-class coach

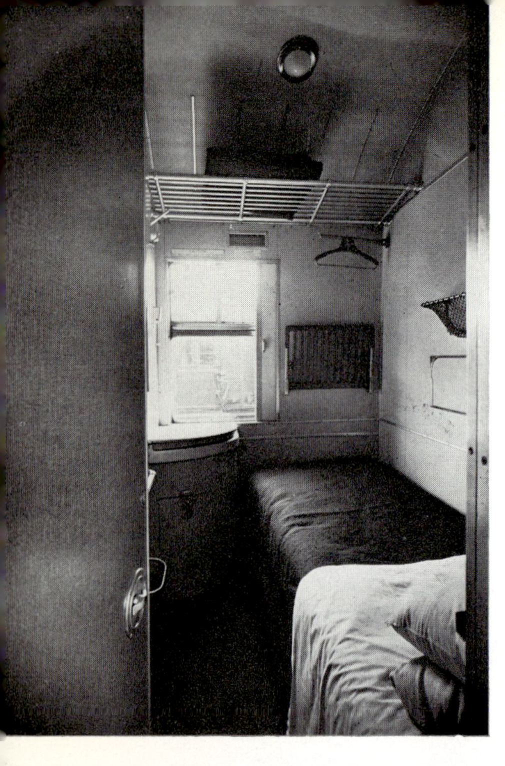

31 (*Left*) View of a first-class sleeping car. Every compartment has a wash basin with constant hot water, shaver point, towels, shoe shine cloth, comfortable bed and reading lamp. A bell summons an attendant with refreshments, and he wakes the passenger in the morning with tea and biscuits

32 (*Below*) British Rail's car-by-train service

33 (*Left*) The Freightliner system of freight transportation uses containers which can be lifted to or from road vehicles and railway wagons

34 (*Below*) A bulk oil train *en route* from an Essex refinery to the Midlands

35 A freight train guard hands over instructions to his driver for a long run through the night

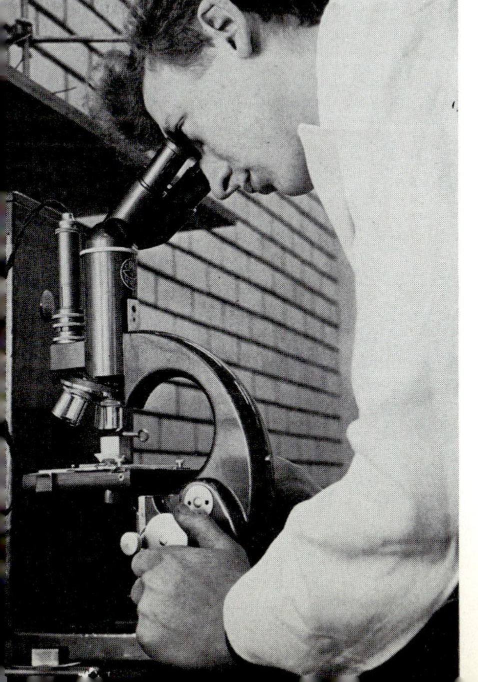

36 (*Above*) At Derby, scientists and technicians work on research projects to make trains more efficient, faster and safer. This shows part of the laboratory where tests on actual locomotives and rolling stock are carried out

37 (*Left*) A scientist at work in one of the laboratories at Derby

38 Model of British Rail's advanced passenger train under development at the Railway Technical Centre, Derby

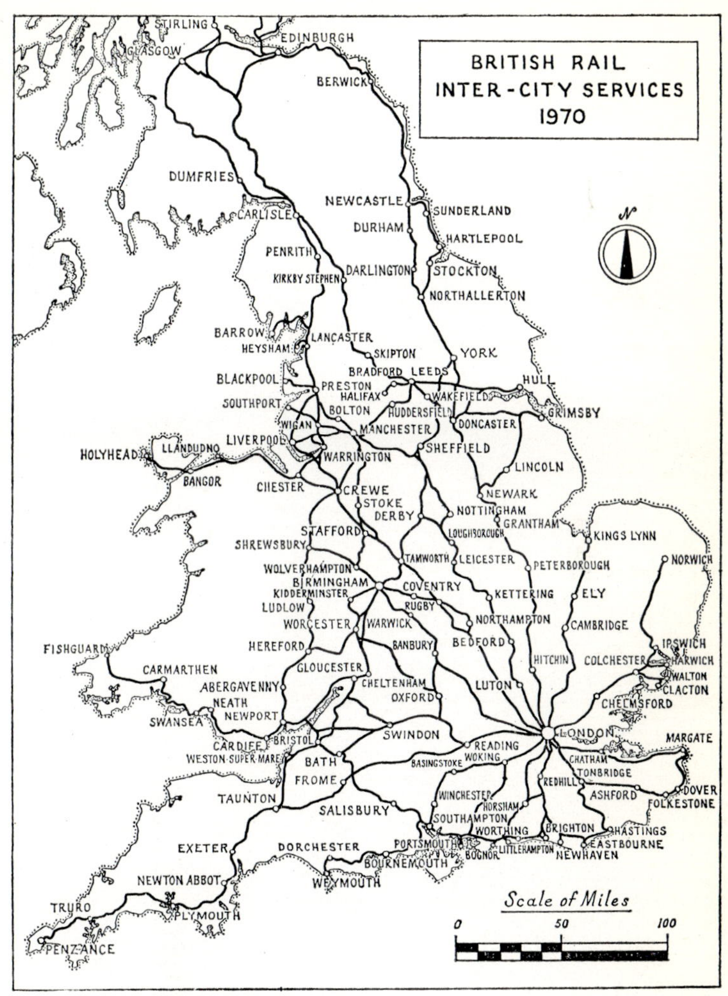

39 Passenger network map. (Reproduced from *Transport Studies*, by John Hibbs, John Baker 1970)

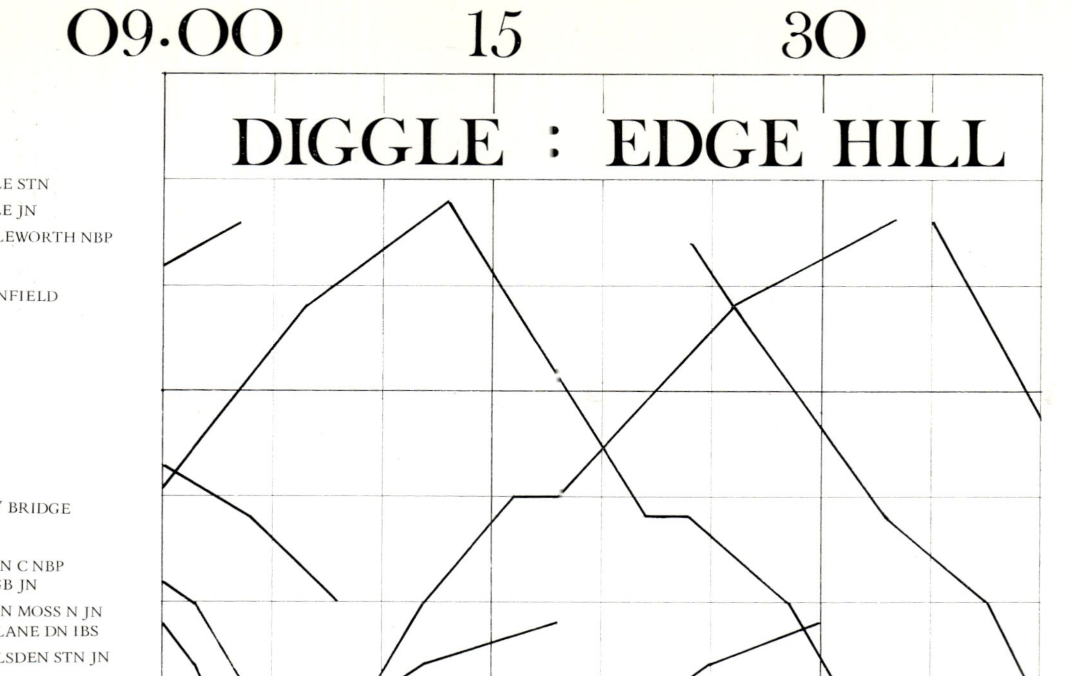

40 A British Rail internal train working graph (timetable)

Glossary of railway terms

ADHESIVE FACTOR The ratio of weight on driving wheels to the nominal tractive effort – the ability to develop maximum power without the wheels slipping on the rails.

A.P.T. Advanced Passenger Train, the registered name for British Rail's proposed 150-m.p.h. passenger train.

BALLAST The layers on which the sleepers are set.

BLANKETING The insertion of layers of material – gravel, sand, ashes, and sometimes concrete – above subsoil, such as clay, which would otherwise work up into the ballast, and cause the rail track to deteriorate.

BLOCK SYSTEM The original system of safe signalling, with a bell code for communication between adjacent signal boxes, and indicators to show whether the line was free, blocked, or a train was actually on the line. The system's principles are embodied in modern signalling methods.

BRAKING SYSTEMS The basic principle of railway braking is that every system shall be 'fail safe'; any parting or mechanical failure automatically applies the brakes. Systems are either vacuum or air operated. On diesel-electric and electric locomotives the motors can also operate as a form of brake, generating current instead of absorbing it.

CATCH POINTS Installed on gradients as a precaution should vehicles break away and begin running backwards.

CATENARY The system for hanging a continuous cable above the track for electrified trains fed by an overhead supply of current.

CENTRALISED TRAFFIC CONTROL The term for remote control of signals and points by electrical systems instead of wires and rods.

CHAIR The seating between the rail and sleeper used on bullhead rails.

CREEP The tendency of rails to move in the direction of the traffic.

DESCRIBER Part of the system to inform signalmen about the identity and route of a train approaching their section.

DETECTOR A device to ensure that the switch blades of facing points fit closely against the rails. Unless they fit and thus complete an electrical circuit the signals cannot be cleared.

FISHPLATE The metal plate bolted to each side of a rail joint. Many rails are today joined by welding, but a large part of track mileage in Britain still has jointed track.

FORMATION The top level of the ground on which the rail bed is built.

FREIGHTLINER High-speed freight train consisting of wagons carrying goods enclosed in containers which can be loaded and off-loaded by mobile cranes and carried by road vehicles.

FROGS Moveable angles installed in a diamond crossing to fill the open space where the rails cross others.

GAUGE The distance, measured between the inner edges of the rails, is the rail gauge – 4 feet 8½ inches in Britain. The load gauge specifies the limits to the dimensions of railed vehicles in order to clear tunnels, railside structures, etc. In Britain there are variations, according to the route involved – London tube railways, for example, obviously having a smaller load gauge than a main line on British Rail.

HORSEPOWER The measurement of the rate of doing work, with one h.p. equal to 33,000 foot pounds per minute. The indicated h.p. of a locomotive is greater than the drawbar h.p. – the power available to move the train because of gravity, mechanical friction, and the weight of the locomotive.

HUNTING The tendency of train wheels to shift from side to side when a curve is taken at speed.

KEY The wooden wedge which holds the rail in position in the chair on old-type bullhead rails.

MARSHALLING YARD The elaborate installation at which freight wagons are assembled or separated as part of trains scheduled for different destinations.

MULTIPLE-UNIT A train without a separate locomotive, but with small motors powering the coaches, thus enabling trains to be long or short, and driven in either direction without shunting.

PACKING The provision of the correct 'top' on the ballast beneath the sleepers.

PLAIN LINE Ordinary railway track without crossings or points.

RETARDER Device worked by an electro-pneumatic mechanism to check the speed of trucks in marshalling yards.

ROUTE INDICATOR A panel on which electric lamps are illuminated to form a figure or letter, operating in conjunction with a signal, at busy junctions and approaches to large stations.

STAFF On single lines, in order to prevent collisions, a staff, or token, was handed to the driver and no train was allowed on the section unless the driver had the staff in his possession. The modern system is for several staffs to be kept, each electronically controlled so that only one staff at a time can be withdrawn. The staff machines also control the signals.

TOP AND LINE Phrase referring to maintenance work – top is the levelling of the rail surface; line refers to alignment of the rails.

TRACTIVE POWER The drawing power of a locomotive, less than the power output. Thus a diesel locomotive of 2,500 h.p. has an output for actual drawing power of around 2,000 h.p. (*see* Horsepower).